Let It Unfold

Let It Unfold

LOVE, LOSS & SURRENDER

POEMS BY S'MARIE YOUNG

To watch video collages and readings of various poems, see back of book for QR scans taking you to shorts including readings of selected poems introduced by the back story of each, or go to the You Tube Playlist, Let it Unfold: https://youtube.com/playlist?list or consciousleadershipinsights.substack.com/s/let-it-unfold

Be sure to subscribe to S'Marie's channel for the latest in poetry, conversations and Conscious Leadership: http://www.youtube.com/@smarieyoung

Cover: Original watercolor by Beth Fountain as as homage to Georgia O'Keeffe Cover and Interior Design and Illustrations by Beth Fountain

Copyright © 2025 by S'Marie Young
Published by S'Marie Young
All rights reserved. No part of this publication may be reproduced, stored in a retrieval system, or transmitted in any form or by any means—electronic, mechanical, photo-copying, recording, casual "snacking", or otherwise—without the express written permission of the publisher. Failure to comply with these terms my expose you to legal action and damages for copyright infringement. Brief quotations embodied in critical articles and reviews are allowed.

ISBN 978-1-7357830-4-8

Library of Congress Control Number: 2025906746

Dedication

In gratitude for this immense
gift, watching it unfold each day.
Thank you my dearest One,
you are the longing in my soul.

Contents

The Pleasures of Doubt	1
Goodbye Uncle	3
Coming Home	4
Ganesh	5
My Dearest One	6
Silence	7
Transitions	8
Sanskrit	9
Celebration	10
Coming Together	11
Fearing God	12
Big Bad Husband	13
Weed Patrol	14
Gross Vibrations	15
Last Night's Dream	16
Ashram Winter Colors	17

Suspended in Ice	18
The Real Thing	19
Air-Mail Home: Fly Free	20
Crossed in the Mail	21
And He Danced	23
Rangolis for Baba	24
Purification Fire	26
Gifts	28
Bindings	29
Eagle Canyon	30
Splitting	31
Only Dust	32
Landing	33
Virgin Mary	35
Yatra	36
Full Circle	38
Change Your Name, Change Your Life	41
Seva Bliss	43
Lingering Questions	45
Darshan	46
Completion	47
Through the Bardo	49
Glossary of Sanskrit and Other Terms	51

Preface

Looking back on my life in a time of huge transition, these poems speak to me today in a way that I recognize as a calling forth of a new way of being in the world. Today, here I am still evolving, always unfolding.

Back then, everything I identified with was slipping away: my 10 year marriage, 25 year career, 18 year old cat, newly remodeled home just as I wanted it to be, friends and community in the desert I loved for 19 years. The years I spent with each bred comfort, familiarity, and sense of security that all fell away at once. These were the elements of my life that gave me a sense of self, of identity.

I've always been a spiritual seeker, although in the beginning it took the form of running away from my Christian roots and from God entirely until I could enter from a new door that felt less confining, where I could form a direct relationship. That led me to a path of meditation, connecting me to the sparkle of divinity within myself, the energy I always knew dwelled in everything and everyone. Now I had a language for it, and a method of relating, and loving it—the vast mystery.

All in all I spent almost a year living a monastic life between four trips to India and one to upstate New York. The silent, structured rhythm of the ashram gave me access to a different part of myself, one that wasn't connected to or dependent on outside trappings that had formed my sense of self. The language of this deeper self is poetry, and it burst forth in a daily outpouring I originally called Ashram Diaries, the book you now have in your hands (or your device).

During these years, there was a wonderful program at Idyllwild Arts school called Poetry Week that I attended four summers, the last two in a chap book group led by poet and professor David St. John. Though his creative guidance, later editing and the synergy of the group, *Let it Unfold* came to life. My deepest gratitude to David.

My original vision was to have the poems illustrated by fellow meditator and artist, Beth Fountain. She finally agreed. My partner and collaborator, I could not have done this book without her.

It took this many years to usher the book out into the world. Time creates a distance, an ability to step away and offer it without personal involvement in the events. Given the current state of upheaval and drastic change in the world, it seems the right time. It has forced me to connect even deeper to my spiritual path, to the practices that have honed me and keep me steady. Though these poems, I hope that sharing my journey of loss and transformation helps you find the stillness within—expanding into the ever-present love that protects and guides you.

Introduction

This series of poems written between 2006 and 2009, reflects a profound journey of spiritual awakening and transformation. Across three trips to India, where I served in an ashram (place of spiritual study and retreat) for a total of seven months, I came to terms with deep personal loss, an identity crisis, grief and surrender. It is a story of spiritual awakening and unfoldment; a journey across the world and to a new life, a new way of being in the world. Whether composed in India, Palm Springs, or Sedona, these poems are infused with the power of grace, the protective force that envelops, sustains and transcends geographical boundaries. Though poetic expression, this collection invites readers into the unfolding of a new life, a new way of being, and the undeniable con-nection between place, spirit, and the healing power of presence.

In the lineage of my path, spiritual power was traditionally passed from one man to another—until it was entrusted to a woman who has carried the strength of the lineage for over forty years. Her living master, who guided her from childhood, prepared her to assume this role. Whether I write to Bade Baba, Baba, or She, they all reflect the same guidance of the wise one that dwells within.

Let It Unfold

LOVE, LOSS & SURRENDER

Pleasures of Doubt

From the Oxford English Dictionary on the usage of Nothing: The whole would be like multiplying nothing by nothing the result would still be nothing.

Stretching out on the lawn in front of the church,
seeds of doubt sprouted inside of me. I don't know
what it was that Pastor Christiansen said that veered me
toward the Red Road; where God is earth, sky, rocks and trees.

Sitting there after confirmation class,
two questions formed in my mind:
*Why were the Native American Indians wrong
in what they believed?* and, *How do you imagine nothing?*

This is how I debunked the creation story that day.
Though I continued attending confirmation class,
I had entered the vast emptiness of atheism.
A proclamation hung on my bedroom wall,

NO GOD in bright blue paint. Small yellow daisies
completed the plaque made by a friend,
who then decided she rather liked wearing a cross
around her neck. I did not graduate and confirm their beliefs.

The blood and bone of Christ never
touched my lips, atoning for my sins.
From those first seeds of doubt I defied generations,
stretching back to the rocky isle of Tofterey,

lying boldly on the North Sea. From where
Monsina Molina Larsdader Toft agreed

to sail for America in her sister's place,
to join her husband to be. Outside the Hovde farm,

in the Gausdal Valley near
Lillehammer, ancestors from
my other side must have shivered
in their churchyard graves.

I don't know how my geography
got so scrambled, but the explanation
I was reaching for was received
by sages in Kashmir, a thousand years before.

Such a long way from Norwegian fjords,
or my grandparents' church on Montezuma
Avenue. The red hymnal weighed heavy in my
hands. Wordy lines crammed into verse,

the organ and my voice would never merge.
My heart sings across another ocean,
a haunting raga calling to me,
moved by tamboura and drums.

Goodbye Uncle

I spent years trying to unravel
my life's great mysteries and what
role you have played. *Why did I follow
in your footsteps, and all my men
become your friend?*

You are gone,
and I don't know any more
now than I did then.

It came to me during an evening chant,
while watching the elephant rain.
It flashed between lines,
*Our karma is done,
whatever it was, it's finished.*

I didn't know then, your time was ending.
After the news, for days I walked in the soft,
thick lushness of the garden,
praying to the symphony of sunlight and raindrops,
that you're passing would be smooth.

Under the canopy of Neem and Mango trees,
soothed by blooming orchids
attached to their trunks; I said goodbye.
Leave it all here,
washed away by monsoon.

Coming Home

I imagined, that last day, while saying goodbye to the Siddhas
that I left you there on a large rock, the one in front of the white
statue of Baba. He's sitting there crossed-legged, meditating next
to a Purple Butterfly Bush, aptly named for the dancing parade
of brilliantly striped winged ones that entertained me each
time I came.

You were curled up in a wicker basket, snuggled
against your favorite blanket, under Baba's loving gaze.
In my mind's eye, I raised a small umbrella, to shield you
from India's intense sun and monsoon rain.

The vet said you would not make it, you were disappearing fast.

Miss Alex, my friend, you've exceeded a cat's nine lives. You'll be
happy here with Baba and the other Siddhas in these sacred
ashram grounds. I left you there with a sad farewell to catch the
long flight.

To my relieved wonderment, you welcomed me home,
dull black and white fur on protruding bones.

A tearful reunion ensued, ending the longest separation
of our shared lives. Now, a year later, you're still here.
When I panic inside each time you don't come to my call,
I fear a coyote got you, or you found a rock to curl under and die.

Then, I remember, you are no longer mine.
I left you in Baba's garden chasing butterflies.

Ganesh

On the road to Mumbai, white cast Ganesh figures line the road.
Ganesh, India's patron deity, you protect my home.
You are only a bronze statue, yet generations have worshipped you.
You faithfully stand guard at my front door.

Ganesh, India's patron deity, you protect my home.
Half elephant, half boy, your big belly makes me laugh, as
you faithfully stand guard at my front door.
Passing your dancing figure, I bubble forth with joy.

Half elephant, half boy, your big belly makes me laugh, as
you are imbued with God's power, I pray for your strength. Passing
your dancing figure, I bubble forth with joy,
placing a red rose in one of your four outstretched hands.

You are imbued with God's power, I pray for your strength; while
giving you oblations my heart fills with grace.
Placing a rose in one of your four outstretched hands,
as remover of ego, I stand before you with downward gaze.

While giving you oblations, my heart fills with grace,
counting my blessings for this fine day.
As remover of ego, I stand before you with downward gaze. On the
road to Mumbai, white cast Ganesh figures line the road.

My Dearest One

With profound pain and longing
I called out to you.
You answered, and here I am.

My life dismantled,
I present myself in disintegration.
An open book, a new script,
create me as you see fit.

A gift I don't yet fathom,
to be in your India home,
nurtured, protected, guided
to see clearly
the ways I close my eyes to you.

The tools of spiritual practice have been given
to delve deeper and deeper within.
It is up to me to use them,
focusing myself on the goal
until my small i is no longer here.

In gratitude for this immense gift,
watching it unfold each day.
Thank you my dearest One,
you are the longing in my soul.

Silence

It is said, the all knowing ones
Become one with everything—
I'm starting with hips and spine.

We chant the name of God
in the predawn,
before the noise of the day.

Sitting cross-legged on the floor,
my hips relax and open,
my spine reaches upward.

I'm getting a sense of the
stillness within, that its one
with the silence in the trees.

Transitions

My new friend left last night,
Returning to her husband and her home office
nestled amidst the pines of Bainbridge Island.

After rooming together
in five days of retreat silence,
we emerged ecstatic on the village streets
of Ganeshpuri and Vajeshwari.

We bowed before Nityananda's Samadhi Shrine
and visited his original home.
We offered flowers to the Devis
and walked the temple gardens
with a busload of curious fifth graders from Mumbai.

Last night, alone in our flat, I re-packed
my suitcase to travel a few buildings away.
My next roommate, by the look of things,
is a woman who padlocks her closet, and
shuts all the windows and doors.

I'll sit on my balcony now,
enjoying a cup of tea.
Quietly celebrating my birthday
at dawn on a new day.

Sanskrit

A mystical language, birthed from
sounds heard by ancient sages
deep in meditation.
Words formed a message
from within.

Seed letters strung together.
Said come to me, come to me.

Celebration

Coming home after Swadhyaya,
just before the first light of day,
tiny blue sparkling lights approach,
against the outline of a big truck cab.

My trip from Mumbai flashes—
surrounded by work trucks, I tried to snap pictures
of the brightly painted wood panels
and doors, scrolled and flowered,
back ends proclaiming, "India is Great!"
"Honk Horn Please!"

A country of celebration, I go to sleep
to loud speakers blaring from Ganeshpuri
a mile away and am awakened in the dark
to sacred recitations broadcasted at full pitch.

A local swami is in the temple square
for an annual ten day chanting fest.
Cars and buses flow in each day,
on a narrow two lane road, built for one rickshaw.

Neighboring villagers camp side by side
with fast moving city dwellers.
United in a pilgrimage to honor the Great One,
the One that reflects the greatness in ourselves.

Coming Together

We arrived here from scattered parts of the globe.
Speaking in numerous dialects, we come together
in the language of the heart.
Converging in this time and place
to work toward a common goal,
to see ourselves and each other as One.

A path of discovery that leads
deep inside to the knowledge
of who we are,
God playing many parts.

Fearing God

Dear Baba, I am afraid
of being alone.
Please, fill me with your love.

You say all I need
is Om Namah Shivaya.
I fear you will take everything

I think I am
and everything I love.
All that's left is you.

I never understood
fearing God. That was a God
I wanted no part of.

Now, trying to merge with you,
I understand.
You are all consuming.

You want all of me.
I am willing, but afraid.
A big part of me won't let go.

May I give you a little piece at a time?

Big Bad Husband

I met a few of my enemies yesterday—
pride, attachment, blame and jealousy.
Just as I opened the door to giving up my home,
its upkeep and responsibilities,

my enemies showed up quickly trying to bar that door,
to keep me from ever walking through.
They put on quite a show, dredging through my deepest fears—
had me in tears by late afternoon.

Fantasy runs unabated- not only leaving my home, but
everything in it, my town, friends and family. My big bad
husband did this to me!
He left me for another woman too, wrote me a letter—couldn't
even do it by phone!

The teachings say to give up desires
and attachments to people and things;
but I don't have to become a sadhu
with only a loincloth and begging bowl.

I can keep what serves me
and allows me to serve. It's those inner enemies
I need to dispose of somehow
gaining control of my mind.

Weed Patrol

My mind wanders like crabgrass
choking out the good thoughts
I plant and tend.

I need round-the-clock
weed patrol, uprooting those wild
offshoots running rampant in my yard.

Those renegades steal all the water
and sunlight leaving no room
for brilliant flowers to bloom.

Gross Vibrations

When I think of an ashram,
beauty, stillness, peace
and serenity comes to mind.

Last night as I went to bed,
an animated conversation
was going on outside,

and in the background
the nightly occupela chant
sang out from the village square.

Dogs chimed in, as a generator
across the street revved up.
Neighbor's activities echo

through concrete walls,
as if they are in the next room.
Old diesel buses with squeaky brakes

pass throughout the day.
I read how Baba would create
irritating situations to

force people to turn within.
A shaman told me before I left
the purpose of my trip to India was

to learn how to stay unaffected by the
gross vibrations of the world.
The lessons go twenty-four hours a day.

Last Night's Dream

We were swimming in the ocean,
relaxing, enjoying the cool water
side by side.

A killer shark swam up next to us,
gray slick back gleaming in the sun.
Brian tried to divert him, make him go away.

I let him approach. Reaching out
to touch that massive jaw,
seeing razor sharp teeth that could

crush me in one bite,
submitting to the process
of being chewed, swallowed,

digested back into the whole.

Ashram Winter Colors

Hong Kong Orchid Tree
hot pink blooms fall to the ground
brightening the earth.

Red whiskered Bul Bul
under lavender bells
flits to a rock bath.

Tiny deer wanders
looking for a luscious bite
of new greenery.

Flame of Forest tree
offering to Sai Baba
vivid orange flowers.

Brown snake slithers by
grey lizard lives in cupboard
already realized.

A magpie Robin
fluffing black and white feathers
on a sparse leaved branch.

Next to Baba sits
Purple Spike Butterfly Bush
attracting winged ones.

Indian Myna
looks at me on the pathway
with yellow rimmed eyes.

Suspended in Ice

Words pop up, stinging like shots from a BB gun.
Too strong, too slow, too hard, too weak,
too cold, like an ice queen.
Every jab, another layer freezes over.

Too strong, too slow, too hard, too weak;
until I'm so numb I can't feel a thing.
every jab another layer freezes over;
this frozen field longs for spring.

Until I'm so numb I can't feel a thing,
staying as if suspended in ice.
This frozen field longs for spring,
for flower shoots and warm muzzles.

Staying as if suspended in ice,
frozen solid with fear of being alone.
For flower shoots and warm muzzles,
take a chance with a meltdown.

Frozen solid with fear of being alone,
a man's wounds become my own.
Take a chance with a meltdown;
please burn away all that's not mine.

A man's wounds become my own,
through a misguided notion of love.
Please burn away all that's not mine,
as words pop up stinging like shots from a BB gun.

The Real Thing

*We met for lunch
at the Cheesecake Factory.
He picked it up on the way.
As I opened my birthday gift,
he warned me that all
but the big rock in the center was real.*

*A disclosure to prevent
an upset over the extravagance.
He said no one would ever know but me.
I don't care how good it looks.
Even if it comes in a smaller package,
I want the real thing.*

To My Husband, Air Mail Letter Home: Fly Free

Raven perched high in a branch,
black feathers glistening in the noonday sun,
wings rustling, restless to spread.

Take flight my dear one,
stretch out and glide with the wind,
find your source of light.
Leave behind this old, familiar date palm grove.

Following the horizon, crest Mt. San Jacinto,
rising ever higher. Cruise towards sunset,
low over the Pacific, as foaming white spray
loosens rough desert sand.

Listen, intuit the dolphins' message.
Trust the pod to guide you
where your heart longs to go.
Find the drum that matches its beat,
in the rhythm of pounding wings.

Search for an air current to catch and soar
'til you reach warm breezes.
Alight on an isle flourishing with coconut palms
and mango trees. Dive deep into translucent waves.
Observe sand and water merge

and separate again, and again.
Fire, water, earth and sky;
may all the elements nurture and sustain,
as you discover your bliss.

Crossed in the Mail

I still care for you, but I have to go.
I'll be moved out
by the time you return,
so you can have the house, as agreed.

NO, you can't move, I made plans!!!

Keep the fabulous kitchen
just finished
earthen-granite-counter-tops
iridescent flecks softly back-lit
burnished maple cabinets
backsplash tiny bronzed glass squares.

Enjoy Saltillo-tiled entry and patio-your gift
after bathing in Hanas' Seven Sister Falls my
surprise entry gate
turquoise and gold rays of sun,
photo replica Sedona home

opening to fragrant night-blooming jasmine
white bougainvillea overhang
soothing water
trickling from lotus petals
at Buddha's crown.

alone
in Balinese-sleigh-bed
no view

morning ritual
naked arc into pool
against date palms
unrelenting blue sky.

No

you can't move!
leave the rainwater shower
you insisted on, or
the super-jet massage-
burning-hot spa,
searching for falling stars?

How about I take
the powder room sink?
smooth glass bowl,
painted
blue-green bamboo.

P.S. Cat goes with house

And He Danced

In memory of Kaka

As the chant built,
drums beat faster, voices rose.
His small frame could no longer contain

the ecstasy bursting from his enormous heart.
Tiny bells around his ankles vibrated
with energy, urging him to motion.

With a slight nod and a smile
from the chair front and center
he leapt from his seat

and danced up the aisle,
hand cymbals and toes
twinkling in joyous abandonment.

Rangolis for Baba

He arrived at two o'clock
in the morning each day
with paintbrushes made of sand,
colored in the palette of the sacred
paradise that he called home.

The flaming orange and bright pink
of the African Tulip and Hong Kong Orchid trees.
Brilliant blues, greens, yellows
and reds of the peacocks and macaws.
Fawnskin and soft grays from all the deer and
Vijay the elephant.

He began at the threshold of the ashram gate,
pouring fine sand in lines forming mandalas
and mystical scenes,
filling in colors as they came.

In the stillness of the night,
his masterpiece emerged and spread,
sometimes spanning ten feet. Across the sidewalk
and into the street; all of a sudden it was done.

He tiptoed across for final touches,
never leaving a smudge. Standing back in amazement at what
lay before him, stunningly beautiful and completely unique.

Soon sleepy residents and guests would walk
through on the way to early morning chants,
staring in wonder at the creation they passed.

As the day progressed, lines and colors blurred
with each step through the gates.

In the afternoon, Kaka, Uncle, would be back
to sweep up the remains, always with joy on his face.
No need to mourn a treasure gone,
for he was only performing these daily tasks
as his Guru asked.

Purification Fire

Everything I was holding on to burned
in the heat of the ashram fire;
I've been granted a new life.
My eighteen-year-old cat was the last,
she died two days ago, but not without saying goodbye.

She came to me in an afternoon nap,
awakening to her soft meow.
As I lay there with closed eyes, I saw the blue pearl,
a pinpoint of divine light that remained steady
within view for the first time.

As Miss Alex was taking her last breaths,
wild cats entered the grounds,
tearing around with high pitched cries.
All was quiet the following day.

Thoughts returned to Kaka's death a few weeks ago.
I heard that he was wrapped in white cloth
and taken for cremation to the bank of the Tansa River nearby.
His ashes were later immersed in sacred waters
of the Godavari River at Trymbakeshwar.

I'll spread her ashes in the mountain waters
of the wash running through Eagle Canyon
in Palm Springs, at the same spot where ashes
of my husband's mother and brother were placed in 2001.

I went to Baba's statue in the garden
and placed a heart shaped garland of fragrant
jasmine on the rock in front of him,
where, two years ago, I prayed to leave her in his care
when I thought she was going then.

Miss Alex you knew
where I'm going
I can't take you

Gifts

Bird calls echo through the trees,
heralding dawn.
The orange flowering bushes
around Ganesh
seem extra bright today.

An energy of excitement fills the air—
could it be coming from me?
I am grateful to be alive
in this Indian paradise,
a mirage shimmering on the stripped
jungle plain of Maharashtra.

One who's image is kept intact
by the guru's intention
and each seeker who comes
to give and receive.

Bindings

I've let go of the big stuff,
the husband, the cat, the house
and the community.
Furniture, china, pots and pans
now occupy my thoughts.
Why do they seem more
difficult to leave behind?

In death or divorce, it's the loose ends,
the strands of attachment
that hold me down.
How quickly I lose my peaceful state
when I reach out to grab.

Release and simplify,
travel lightly into the next life.
All that baggage in storage
for some future date
will bind me tighter than rope.

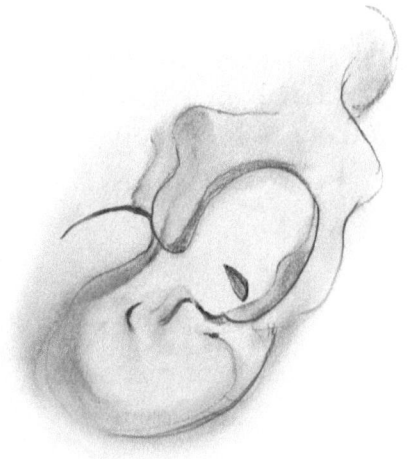

Eagle Canyon

Over a centerpiece of wormed cactus wood, covered in brilliant blooms, I held a fresh-picked bouquet of lupine, verbena, and desert marigolds, as we vowed to each other to share our lives. We were blessed—an awakening given by our guru's grace. Lakshmi, the goddess of abundance, showered us with gifts, and cleared the debts of our past.

A few debts remained, however, one's that would have to be lived out. Old demons lay in wait, poking out their ugly heads at inopportune times. We learned to react in different ways—a conscious rerun of old relationships you might say. Here we are at the finale. Life has come to collect; for you can't outrun a karmic debt. The fire of Kundalini Shakti burns most, but there are some you must repay.

Sharing a good life
One final lesson for us
Let go see what's next

Goodbye and thank you. I carry no regrets.
As we begin our separate lives, please know, we fully completed what we were brought together to do.

Splitting

We reached a crossroads unaware.
He went to Las Vegas,
I went to India.

The road had split long before,
but somehow we imagined
we walked side by side.

Now, separated by land
and water, we finally saw
we were oceans apart.

We looked at one another
with great compassion
and wished for each the best.

I bowed and left to the sound
of temple bells as he turned
and climbed the penthouse stairs.

Only Dust

Early June, I took the bag containing Miss Alex's ashes out of its cedar box. Placing it carefully in my fanny pack, I drove through old Palm Springs, to Eagle Canyon, the Earth Mother's home. As towering Father Mountain looked on, I slowly walked into the mouth of her womb, up the familiar path, stopping at meditation rock to offer a prayer, allowing her presence to be felt.

Amidst crackling scrub and prickly cactus, playing dead for the sweltering months ahead, I looked for an animal trail to take me to an entrance to the cascading rocks in the now-dry wash. All overgrown, trampling through stickery grass, finding only dead ends at sharp drops. Reaching a boulder overlooking granite falls, I dropped some ashes into a protected crevice, and left, respectful that entrance had been denied.

Finding my way to a small finger of the wash; it was easy climbing down to soft sand. Reaching into the bag, releasing thick ashes, letting it sift through my fingers and float in the wind. With each handful, heart bubbles broke loose and sailed along. Pieces of me powdered and returned to earth, as if performing my own last rites.

dusty fingers rest
against upper lip breathe deep
savor cedar smell.

Landing

Standing alone in an empty soccer field at Christmastime,
tears streaming down my face
I gaze at Tahquitz Peak rising before me,
snow drifting down the mountain to meet me halfway.

My first symbol of God, discovered two decades before,
his afternoon shadow not yet
engulfing me and the desert floor.
With resignation, I ask him what I've done
to make him done with me.

My master's words came flooding back,
when she came here thirteen years ago and captured me.
The desert is very particular,
it doesn't let just anyone live here.
Definitely, it will let you know when it's time to leave.

After she left, she visited me in a dream,
with smug attitude, I said—
What's she doing knocking at my door?
I didn't know then I needed her;
it took a year more before I was willing
to let her rescue me.

My almost-ex and other friends said I was brave and
crazy to go. Wear sunglasses and a head-scarf for a midnight
landing in Mumbai.
Tall, blond, and blue-eyed—there's just no way to blend in.
The frozen terror of December 2008 from the Taj and Oberoi
highlighting the blue and blond.

After waiting for luggage over an hour
wheeling bags out of immigration,
face flushed from a yellow turtleneck underneath,
I emerge in a sea of friendly, brown male faces,
moist with warmth and the Arabian Sea.
Head held high, no fear around; I greet my driver,
Please, just take me home.

Virgin Mary

In a dream last night,
my husband hung this on the wall:
A floor-length-midnight-blue-velvet dress,
a pearl brooch setting off the high neck.

Encircled by luminous blue-black beads,
it was a costume for the Queen—
and I am more like Mary Magdalene.

So why did I marry two Irish-Catholic boys?
The chasm I could never bridge
between Virgin and Christ's defiled Bride
until Parvati appeared in my life.

Shiva's consort, Kundalini manifest,
pure, luminous, sensual,
divine Mother of all.

Yatra

I

Small fires burn curbside,
lighting the street,
long before sunrise.
Men huddle close,
warming their hands,
waiting for smokestack buses
to haul them to local brick factories
and construction sites in Mumbai.

After four hours of driving through sleepy villages
and brown hills,
the dry landscape
turns lush green.
Miles and miles of vineyards and onion rows,
dotted with tiny temples and mosques;
for the farmer in the field.

Life is worship.
Deities oversee the crops;
rain is exchanged
for offerings of marigolds.

We are traveling to a one-room hut,
to meditate under a mango tree,
listen to birds sing and an old,
wrinkled sadhu repeating
Om Namah Shivaya.

To sit where our Baba sat,
some sixty years ago
fully absorbed in his journey
to the inner realms.

In the center of the room,
his wooden sandals on a tray,
adorned with red hibiscus,
freshly picked.

II.
A few more hours by car,
a billboard welcomes us.
Come to Shirdi, home of Sai Baba
and a water park.

Indians from afar
travel to offer a garland
or rose bouquet
and pray for a miracle
from the compassionate one.
They bow, heads to floor,
before his *mahasamadhi* hrine.

In a burlap bag, our shoes
sit on a shelf piled with thousands of others.
Barefooted on hot sidewalk,
we make our way to the queue.

Across turnstiles and bag checks,
the line slowly moved
against blowing fans,
through four giant halls,
front to back, snaking all walls.

Just three milk faces, immersed
in a dark honey pot, surrounded
by saris, whispers and soft singing.

Reaching the inner sanctum,
we gaze at his perfect image, seated on a throne,
and long to touch the silver sandals, embedded
in the marble encasement
under which his feet lay.

Offering rupees and obeisance
through Plexiglas,
we receive fragrant flowers as prasad.

Wandering through the museum
and grounds, we see the tree
under which he lived
until his final merging
in nineteen-eighteen.
A late lunch of delicious veg-Korma and rice,
creeping down ashram
walkways at midnight,
sure to sleep
through four-o'clock temple bells.

Full Circle

Having left behind
Siddhartha a book I loved
nature abhors void

As a young adult, my bible became
Think and Grow Rich.

Faithfully reading aloud as instructed
daily recitation of a handwritten goal—
the largest income possibly conceived.
Year after year, tenaciously repeating,
the goal was finally reached.

Browsing ashram shelves
surprising source of wisdom
quote from a Yankee

in *Devatma Shakti, Kundalini Divine,* written in 1948 by an Indian monk:
> *Napoleon Hill,* in Think and Grow Rich
> *says that sexual energy can be transmuted*
> *to higher creative energies of science, art and*
> *poetry…transmutation of sexual energy can*
> *easily make one develop in him or her the "sixth sense",*
> *inner voice of inspiration and divine communication.*

Having been liberated by women of the sixties,
I ignored Hill's suggestion of sexual sublimation.

> *A yogi does not stop there,*
> *but with full determination, proceeds on*
> *to reach the top of full evolution of self.*

My twelve-year-old mind
channeled the yogi writer
opposite result

There's no God because
something can't come from nothing—
he says that there is!

> *Something cannot come out of nothing,*
> *therefore we are led to believe*
> *that fundamental electronic particles*
> *are formed of some cosmic energy possessing*
> *life…either reflecting life itself*
> *or a form of the life principle.*

Life is created from one's very perspective.
Learning from years of daily reading that
old dry statement, that no desire
worth its achievement comes outside the heart…

Full evolution
when heart merges with the One
all those desires flee.

Change Your Name...Change Your Life

Recently, I heard that old cliché for the first time.
Had I known, would I still have done it?
I didn't even change the whole thing, just combined
the first letter of the first name with the middle name—

does that really qualify for such a complete makeover?
There's not much left to recognize as me.

When you turned the Palm Springs Convention Center
into an ashram for a three-week winter retreat;
curious, I visited twice. The first time I laid eyes on you,
we passed in an empty hallway and you said hello,
reading the nametag stuck to my chest.

My next visit, I stood in a long line
to bow before your chair on New Year's Eve,
arguing inside how foolish it was the whole time.
Then, when I couldn't move or stop staring;
you handed me a box of chocolates,
as your giant peacock feather wand gently brushed me along.

I ate those chocolates, and poof,
in just over a year, all my dreams came true.
And eleven years later...poof and it's gone.

I visited your home last summer, in the Catskills of New York.
You appeared after so many years,
my longing to see your form unquenched,
still mirthful, yet unmistakably fierce.

In a roomful of people, you asked my name;
not really hearing my reply. No matter–

you know who I am from the inside out,
past, future, beyond time, place and name.

You see that it's all just a game of the mind,
and I take it so seriously.
My teacher, my friend, all future moves,
I surrender to you.

Seva Bliss, a Booklist Poem*

Stillness speaks through the roomful
of donated books I dust each day,
one shelf at a time. I asked for wonder
and the presence of God, and you gave me
a dusting cloth.

The wonder that is India is the chasm of fire
I dive into each time I'm here. I've taken a thousand
journeys, yet have been to only one
of the holy places and temples of India.

I asked how to know God and whispers
from eternity directed me down the path of no self.
Practicing the supreme yoga, I have been surprised
by joy and the power of compassion.

A holy man told me in the Song of the Siddhas
that the splendor of recognition is the dance of Shiva,
the divine player within myself. I've experienced his animating
energy– the triumph of the goddess, Kundalini,
and have felt a shift in the wind.

I accept this gift as part of God's rainbow, knowing
that Shiva and Shakti are mirrors
of the soul within,
the eyes of the world.

This is the yoga of supreme identity, a discovery
of the inner life, transformed by love.
It leads to the truth of the enlightened heart:
I am a divine light in a divine body.

My burning heart created this longing that sent me
on the pilgrimage through this drunken universe, singing
a naked song, searching for the serpent power, the nectar
of self awareness, uttering a common prayer:

Let me live my life in abandonment to divine providence,
cloaked in a garland of divine flowers,
seeing only light upon light.

*there are 43 book titles in this poem

Lingering Questions

After five days of uttering only
a few necessary words,
silence runs deep.

*How can I preserve and pack it
to the other side of the world?*

Receiving holy water,
drinking from my palm
anointing third-eye, crown and heart.

Knees and forehead touch the earth,
praying for loved ones,
May I leave them in Your care?

More than anything,
I miss my home...
*Why did you get the home-life I wanted
and I became the wanderer you were going to be?*

Darshan

In the village of Parvati's son,
sits Bangalore Sanatorium,
where Bade Baba spent his last days.

I sat upstairs in a large window-lined room,
empty but for his shrine; next to the room
where the *avadhut*'s soul
rode out on the last breath,
never again to assume physical form.

Cross-legged on a floor-cushion,
back against a pillow on the wall,
amidst the sounds of a Black Crow's caws,
and mid-morning street bustle below,

eyes closed, head and shoulders
irresistibly dropped,
his presence softly vibrating,
alive in my heart.

Completion

Wrapped in a cocoon of love
gestation is complete.
In a few days I'll re-enter
the other side of the world,

landing as a brand new being
emerged from several layers
of old skin.

Feeling closer than ever
to the Source, may I always live
from the center of my being.
When feelings of emptiness arise,
may I take the path that leads within,
and fill my cup from there.

May I always be grounded
in the feet of my guru.
May every word and action
emanate from the blue pearl,
as a reflection of her unconditional love.

No matter where in the world I am,
may I live from the heart
of Ganeshpuri.

Through The Bardo

Driving into Boynton Canyon in Sedona, Arizona,
home to the Clovis people thousands of years ago;
I am entering sacred space, a timeless dimension.

A premonition comes to me; as it did years ago,
hiking around Bell Rock. *You will die here one day.*
And recognition– today is that day;
death to my dreams and illusions.

The wind swirls around me,
entering the canyon, walking on red earth.
The ancient spire looms ahead.
Ascending the red rock, the trees sing out,
whistling a high pitch.

Circling the spire, finding the ledge
where I travel in my meditations,
overlooking the vast green valley below.
Red spires dot the landscape clear to the horizon,
a gray, luminous sky overhead.

Gazing out and within, offering a prayer:
May I live the rest of my days in each present moment,
savoring it as if the last. I surrender to earth and sky,
offering myself as I am. Empty me and leave a shell,
to replenish and serve your will.

eyes opening wide
a new rangoli each day
colored the rainbow

Glossary of Sanskrit and Other Terms

ASHRAM:
Place of spiritual study and retreat.

BABA:
Respected father, an endearing term for a male guru or saint.

BADE BABA:
Senior Baba.

BARDO:
The in-between place one goes after death, can be a place of disillusionment and disappointment.

BLUE PEARL:
a tiny point of blue light that is the divine energy sometimes seen in meditation.

DARSHAN:
In the presence of a great being.

MAHASAMADHI: When a Realized Being leaves his body for a final merging with God and will not longer reincarnate.

OM NAMAH SHIVAYA:
a sacred mantra, meaning I bow to the Lord within myself.

PARVATI'S SON:
Ganesh, half man, half elephant. The patron saint of India. Protector and destroyer of ego.

RED ROAD:
Native American spiritual path.

SADHU:
a wandering renunciate, who's only possessions are a loincloth and begging bowl.

SERPENT POWER:
Kundalini Shakti.

SEVA:
selfless service.

SHAKTI:
animating spiritual energy of the universe

SWADHYAYA:
chanting sacred texts.

YATRA:
A pilgrimage to a sacred place.

Let It Continue to Unfold
Beyond the page, the journey deepens...

There's a whole different experience when you listen to the poems, hear the backstory and watch them come alive on video. A big thanks to Lexi McPherson Wade who designed the creative video sequences accompanying my readings of the poems. Please scan below:

 *Let it Unfold* Playlist on YouTube (includes many short clips): (*Let it Unfold* YOUTUBE playlist)

 Let it Unfold Playlist on Substack: (Let it Unfold Substack Section)

Individual Poems

 And He Danced

 Let It Unfold Introductory Post (Silence)

 Ashram Winter Colors

 Celebration

 Bindings

 Weed Patrol

 Silence

 Transitions

About S'Marie Young

As a certified coach, S'Marie infuses every client engagement with a powerful blend of presence-centered listening, creative insight, and strategic guidance. With 30 years of experience in meditation and self-development, she shares her professional, life, and spiritual wisdom in her award winning book, Emergence: A Path to Presence. This guide helps readers stand powerfully in their truth while living fully in each moment.

S'Marie lives with her husband by the cliffs overlooking the Pacific Ocean in San Diego, California.

www.ingramcontent.com/pod-product-compliance
Lightning Source LLC
Chambersburg PA
CBHW020547080526
44583CB00013B/1038